I0531243

SPIRITUAL BLISS

An Expression of Love

JOHN BILTI

Library of Congress Control Number (LCCN): 9798902240303

ISBNs:
eBook: 979-8-90224-029-7
Paperback: 979-8-90224-030-3
Hardback: 979-8-90224-031-0

Published by:
Authors Publishing House
178 Broadway, 3rd Floor, #1343
New York, NY 10001, USA

Main Line: (855) 624-0155
Email: support@authorspublishinghouse.com

The book analyzes the concepts of "Come and Go", providing a detailed examination of the underlying principles that connect these templates.

The book contains evangelism templates and guidelines on how to "Meet people where they're at".

This book extends beyond a standard curriculum by integrating personal spiritual experiences, offering a framework that readers may also adopt in their own development.

Who is to read this book?

"Everyone who accepted Jesus as Lord and Savior must read this book!"

"How much do you have to hate somebody to believe that everlasting life is possible and not tell them that?"

Penn Jillette

Table of Contents

About the Author

John Bilti has a profound passion for serving in God's Kingdom by leading people to Christ. He has been married to Claudia for over 33 blessed years. Together, they have raised three children: Ramona, Andrea, and John Andrew, all of whom are now married. At a young age, John began his journey as a youth and worship leader, dedicating himself to investing in and guiding others to serve Christ Jesus and His Kingdom. He has pursued various educational paths, earning a degree as a Web Development Specialist from the Institute of Technology in 2003, studying Biblical Studies at a Bible university in 2012, and obtaining a certification as a Human Resource Project Manager from the American Academy of Project Management in 2021. In 2006, John was ordained as a Pastor at Hope Romanian Baptist Church in Sacramento, CA, where he served as Senior Pastor and Associate Pastor at Grace Romanian Baptist Church in Sacramento. Additionally, John has played a vital role in planting three churches in Washington, California, and Nevada. Alongside his pastoral responsibilities within a Romanian Baptist congregation, John led the Romanian Baptist Association of the U.S. and Canada for six years as President of the Mission Board. He is the co-founder and current president of Impact Global Network Ministry (ignministry.com). John Bilti currently serves Crossroads Church of Jackson County, Jefferson, as Mission Pastor as well as Consultant and Coach at Impact Disciples.

John Bilti has always had a passion to express his love for God and his love of people by equipping believers to engage their world with the Gospel of Good News. This text will equip you to fulfill the mission that Christ has given each believer: as you go, make disciples.

Peter Kendrick, ThD
Retired Professor of Theology and Culture
New Orleans Baptist Theological Seminary

John Bilti is a passionate, thoughtful, and biblically driven evangelist and disciple maker! This book is a clear testimony to that fact! If it's your desire to be the same, then reading and studying this book will be an enormous assistance to get you there!! So read, absorb, and practice!!

Phil Roberts
Director of International Theological Education – GMF,
Former President of Midwestern Baptist Seminary,
Former Vice President of the North American Mission Board

Spiritual Bliss: An Expression of Love by John Bilti is a practical guide every Christian should read. If you've felt stuck in your faith or unsure how to share the gospel, this book will help you move forward.

John addresses a real problem in today's church. Too many believers have become comfortable Christians who avoid talking about faith unless necessary. This book challenges that mindset and shows a better way through the Come and Go framework, a clear pathway with four stages:

Come and See, Come and Follow, Come and Remain, and Come and Go Out. Each stage builds on the last, moving from curiosity to active witness. The book includes helpful diagrams and charts that make these concepts easy to understand and apply.

What makes this book different is its emphasis on meeting people where they are. John shows us how to share faith with compassion and authenticity, just as Jesus walked among people and spoke truth in love. Every point is grounded in Scripture, and he writes with pastoral warmth and honesty, sharing what he's learned through decades of ministry.

This book is for anyone who wants to grow in faith and learn to share it with others. Whether you're a new believer or seasoned Christian, you'll find practical tools and biblical wisdom here. If you're ready to move from passive belief to active discipleship, read this book and put it into practice.

Mark Hobafcovich

National Director of Multiethnic and

Training at the North American Mission Board

Introduction

Evangelism is fundamentally rooted in the reception of divine love as exemplified through Christ Jesus and signifies the active dissemination of this love to others. This study asserts that evangelism serves as both a theological imperative and a practical demonstration of Christian compassion, reflecting the transformative influence of God's love on individual and communal levels.

John 3:16 "For God so loved the world that He gave His only begotten Son, that whoever believes in Him should not perish but have everlasting life."

The deliberate decision to withhold the proclamation of the gospel from those who have not yet embraced the Christian faith may be interpreted as an act of self-interest, as it denies others access to the transformative and redemptive message, which is central to Christianity. Conversely, the act of sharing the gospel not only fosters spiritual growth and maturity within the believer but also serves as a tangible expression of Christlike love and obedience. Furthermore, faithfully communicating this message aligns with the biblical mandate to participate in God's redemptive mission and, according to scriptural testimony, results in divine approval and rejoicing.

The mandate to make disciples constitutes a central mission commanded by Jesus to all believers and serves as the foundational purpose of the church.

Evangelism initiates the process and acts as a catalyst for disciple-making.

This book presents practical steps designed to facilitate personal development in alignment with the teachings and example of Jesus.

Chapter One
Counterintelligence

Every story begins somewhere, and so does this one. As an ordained minister, community leader, husband, father, and grandfather, I looked to communicate with my peers in more than words. Many Christ followers still believe they should use words only if necessary.

If this principle were universally applied, a diverse range of professions such as carpenters, artisans, fishermen, and physicians would predominate. The current divergence in the twenty-first century prompts examination of potential influences that may have diverted Christian communities from the foundational teachings of Jesus and His disciples.

This book returns to where the story of a fully Man and fully God began a redemption plan for a lost and sinful world.

I titled this chapter "Counterintelligence" to explore the lost or altered connection of the original story.

This analysis defines spiritual counterintelligence by its main objectives, methods, and applications, drawing on guidance from the Bible as a divinely inspired source.

MAIN OBJECTIVES

Identify Threats!

Witnessing is often the first objective to be overlooked or discouraged.

This remains a significant concern among Christ followers, rooted in human nature.

While this may seem critical, it is important to consider Jesus' perspective on witnessing.

John the apostle picks up the story when Jesus was brought before Pilate and pressed to answer if He is a King.

John 18:37.

"Then Pilate said to him, "So you are a king?" Jesus answered, "You say that I am a king. For this purpose, I was born and for this purpose I have come into the world—to bear witness to the truth. Everyone who is of the truth listens to my voice."

The statement that Jesus made has a profound implication for all who claim to be Jesus' followers. What this is saying is that if you are of the truth, you are to listen to His voice. When Jesus empowers you to do something, you'd better act immediately in obedience and reverence.

Practical steps to listen and act on Jesus' voice include setting aside time daily for prayer, actively seeking ways to serve others in your community, and sharing your faith with those around you with sincerity and love. Jesus, before ascending to His Father, goes beyond telling His disciples to listen; He tells them to do what is asked.

Acts 1:8.

"But you will receive power when the Holy Spirit has come upon you, and you will be my witnesses in Jerusalem and in all Judea and Samaria, and to the end of the earth."

Lukewarm churches and preachers have neglected the importance of witnessing God's truth to the world, posing a threat to new believers.

In early 2000, I visited Romania, where I was born and raised, to participate in an evangelistic outreach, aiming to reach people with the gospel of Christ by going house to house and engaging on the streets. Surprisingly, a local pastor expressed discomfort with this approach, saying:

"We would look like Jehovah's Witnesses, and we won't be welcome."

As a Christ follower, I saw a potential threat to effective outreach as soon as he spoke. I asked how he or church members reached unreached people to bring them into the family of God. The response was typical and reflected a common approach in many churches: members invite their friends to church, where the word of God is preached. I do not fault this approach, but I notice it often leads to a lack of intentional equipping for church members to engage with people outside traditional settings. This limitation can affect the church's mission and growth, as it may hinder deeper connections with unreached individuals and reduce opportunities for transformative discipleship. Every believer should be fully equipped not only to witness but also to grow as committed disciples. I do not blame the pastor or the church alone for this shortcoming, but see it as a broader challenge within church practice.

We learn from the apostle Paul that witnessing in church alone is not enough.

We find his approach in Acts 17:17:

"So he reasoned in the synagogue with the Jews and the devout persons, and in the marketplace every day with them that met him."

In conclusion, what was missing in this true story was the mandate that Jesus gave His church and its leaders, and that is, "Go and make Disciples of all Nations".

Even though there are many seminars and teachings available on how to reach the unreached, I highly recommend contacting Impact Disciple Ministries and asking for the Disciple Making Church seminar and Disciple Making Pastor resources.

It's essential to be more than just a sentimental Christian; we must embrace a genuine passion for reaching the lost. As passionate followers of Christ, we should actively seek opportunities to bear witness to His truth. Encourage yourself by taking practical steps such as engaging in community outreach, participating in Bible study groups, and nurturing your prayer life. By doing so, you'll feel empowered and supported on your spiritual journey, just as Christ did when He walked among us.

Word of God has not changed.

We live in a time of uncertainty, but not discouraged and not without hope. The Bible teaches us that false teachers will infiltrate among us, and we are to stand strong. Jesus gave us a promise regarding His word. We find these words in Matthew 24:35

"Heaven and earth shall pass away, but my words shall not pass away."

Distortion of the word of God is visible, happening all around us. In Psalm 119, we not only find a way not to sin but a way to preserve the word of God. We find the ingredient in verse 11.

"Thy word have I laid up in my heart, That I might not sin against thee."

Memorizing the word of God is an unbelievable tool to preserve it and to keeping you safe from trespassers. It's about internalizing truth so that it shapes our decisions, actions, and even our thoughts.

Meditating brings delight in your life. Psalm 1:2

"But his delight is in the law of Jehovah; And on his law doth he meditate day and night."

The Holy Spirit is to guide you and help you apply the word of God.

John 16:13

"Howbeit when he, the Spirit of truth, is come, he shall guide you into all the truth: for he shall not speak from himself; but what things soever he shall hear, these shall he speak: and he shall declare unto you the things that are to come."

That divine guidance brings both comfort and clarity in times of confusion or uncertainty.

The more we intentionally focus on God's Word, whether through memorization, meditation, or simply listening to the Spirit, the more we are able to stand firm in the face of falsehood and uncertainty.

Equipping yourself with the armor of God is more than just an ability to protect yourself; you are witnessing the Word of God. So many times, in life, we don't match our talk with our walk. For that reason, we create a state of confusion among our peers. Even in difficult circumstances, stay true to who you are in Christ. Paul speaks in Ephesians chapter six to put on the armor of God.

Ephesians 6:10-20.

10 Finally, be strong in the Lord and in the strength of his might. 11 Put on the whole armor of God, that you may be able to stand against the schemes of the devil. 12 For we do not wrestle against flesh and blood, but against the rulers, against the authorities, against the cosmic powers over this present darkness, against the spiritual forces of evil in the heavenly places. 13 Therefore take up the whole armor of God, that you may be able to withstand in the evil day, and having done all, to stand firm. 14

Stand therefore, having fastened on the belt of truth, and having put on the breastplate of righteousness, 15 and, as shoes for your feet, having put on the readiness given by the gospel of peace. 16 In all circumstances take up the shield of faith, with which you can extinguish all the flaming darts of the evil one; 17 and take the helmet of salvation, and the sword of the Spirit, which is the word of God, 18 praying at all times in the Spirit, with all prayer and supplication. To that end, keep alert with all perseverance, making supplication for all the saints, 19 and also for me, that words may be given to me in opening my mouth boldly to proclaim the mystery of the gospel, 20 for which I am an ambassador in chains, that I may declare it boldly, as I ought to speak.

This passage from Ephesians 6:10-20 is a powerful metaphor about spiritual strength and the "armor of God" for Christians. It describes various components of the armor and how they contribute to standing firm against spiritual forces.

Armor of God Chart (Ephesians 6:10-20)

Armor Piece	Symbolism / Spiritual Purpose
Belt of Truth	Represents truth and honesty, the foundation for everything.
Breastplate of Righteousness	Represents moral integrity and the righteousness that comes from God.

Shoes of the Gospel of Peace	Represents readiness and willingness to spread the message of peace.
Shield of Faith	Protects from the attacks of doubt and evil, strengthening trust in God.
Helmet of Salvation	Protects the mind, signifying the security of salvation and the hope of eternal life.
Sword of the Spirit	Represents the Word of God, used for spiritual defense and offense.
Prayer	Continuous communication with God is essential for strength and perseverance.

This chart highlights the different aspects of spiritual armor described by Paul, emphasizing how each part works together for a Christian's protection and readiness to face spiritual challenges.

Disrupt False Teachings

Pilate, after questioning and listening to Jesus' answer, asked another question; What is truth? As he was asking this question, he went outside and made a statement:

"I find no guilt in Him!"

You see, in Jesus' time, there were plenty of false teachers and leaders, and if you think it's different today, think again. We live in a compromised world, and the church is no different. Just because you are telling the truth, it does not mean you won't face persecution and intimidation. Why? Because just like yesteryear, false leaders are among us. We have to restore the fundamentals of church leadership and speak the truth.

Apostle Paul tells his disciple Titus the qualifications for church leaders. In Titus chapter one, Paul reminded Titus that he was left in Crete for a good reason. From verses five to sixteen, he lays out what an elder should look like. I want to mention verse nine:

Titus 1:9

He must hold firm to the trustworthy word as taught, so that he may be able to give instruction in sound doctrine and also to rebuke those who contradict it.

To conclude our Main Objectives, let's remember this: we cannot sit back and be passive. Now is not the time for silence or hesitation; it's the time to rise and be bold! If you are a witness for Jesus, stand tall and be confident, knowing that He is not just a king, He is *the King of Kings and the Lord of Lords!*

We are called to protect God's Word by putting on the full armor of God, especially in a world that tries to weaken and dismiss the power of Scripture. We must stand strong, speak truth boldly, and never compromise. Let us not be swayed by false teachings, but instead, be the ones who disrupt them with truth and love.

As we reflect on these objectives, I urge you to live like Jesus, love like Jesus, and walk like Jesus. He is our perfect example in both what we say and how we live. So go forth with courage, conviction, and compassion, knowing that the King Himself goes before you!

The following chart summarizes the main objectives.

LIVING BOLDLY FOR THE KING OF KINGS

BE BOLD AND ACTIVE	Now is not the time for silence or hesitation, rise and be bold. • Stand tall as a witness for Jesus • Speak with confidence and conviction
DECLARE CHRIST'S SOVEREIGNTY	Jesus is not just a king — He is King of Kings and Lord of Lords. • Proclaim His authority and lordship • Live as His representative
PROTECT GOD'S WORD	Guard Scripture against distortion or dismissal. • Put on the full armor of God • Stand firm in truth
SPEAK TRUTH IN LOVE	Resist false teachings with both truth and compassion. • Confront deception with grace • Model Christlike love while defending truth
LIVE, LOVE, AND WALK LIKE JESUS	Jesus is the perfect example for word and deed. • Emulate His humility and compassion • Let actions reflect His character
MOVE FORWARD WITH COURAGE	The King Himself goes before you — you're never alone. • Step out in faith • Lead with conviction and peace

Be Bold and Active:

- **Hebrews 13:6** "So we can confidently say, The Lord is my helper; I will not fear; what can man do to me?"

- **Ephesians 6:19** "Pray also for me, that whenever I speak, words may be given me so that I will fearlessly make known the mystery of the gospel,"

- **Acts 6:8-10** "[8] Now Stephen, a man full of God's grace and power, performed great wonders and signs among the people. [9] Opposition arose, however, from members of the Synagogue of the Freedmen (as it was called), Jews of Cyrene and Alexandria, as well as the provinces of Cilicia and Asia, who began to argue with Stephen. [10] But they could not stand up against the wisdom the Spirit gave him as he spoke."

Declare Christ's Sovereignty:

- **Isaiah 46: 9-10** "Remember the former things, those of long ago; I am God, and there is no other; I am God, and there is none like me.[10] I make known the end from the beginning, from ancient times, what is still to come. I say, 'My purpose will stand, and I will do all that I please."

- **2 Timothy 1:12** "That is why I am suffering as I am. Yet this is no cause for shame, because I know whom I have believed, and am convinced that he is able to guard what I have entrusted to him until that day."

- **Colossians 2:19** "They have lost connection with the head, from whom the whole body, supported and held together by its ligaments and sinews, grows as God causes it to grow."

Protect God's Word:

- **1 Corinthians 4:6** "Now, brothers and sisters, I have applied these things to myself and Apollos for your benefit, so that you may learn from us the meaning of the saying, 'Do not go beyond what is written." Then you will not be puffed up in being a follower of one of us over against the other."
- **Ephesians 6:11** "Put on the full armor of God, so that you can take your stand against the devil's schemes."

Speak Truth in Love:

- **Ephesians 4:15** "Instead, speaking the truth in love, we will grow to become in every respect the mature body of him who is the head, that is, Christ."
- **Ephesians 4:29** "Do not let any unwholesome talk come out of your mouths, but only what is helpful for building others up according to their needs, that it may benefit those who listen."

Live, Love, and Walk Like Jesus:

- **Philippians 1:6** "being confident of this, that he who began a good work in you will carry it on to completion until the day of Christ Jesus."

- **Luke 3:35** "But love your enemies, do good to them, and lend to them without expecting to get anything back. Then your reward will be great, and you will be children of the Most High, because he is kind to the ungrateful and wicked."

Move forward with Courage:

- **Luke 12:7** "Indeed, the very hairs of your head are all numbered. Don't be afraid; you are worth more than many sparrows."
- **Romans 8:28** "And we know that in all things God works for the good of those who love him, who have been called according to his purpose.

METHODS

Information

People may come in contact with you or want to be part of your inner circle. Information is a great method to analyze the whereabouts, scope, and intentions. They might have different targets than you do. Communicating your identification will make people feel comfortable, uncomfortable, or offended.

I have to confess that it is not always comfortable to reveal your identification as a Christ follower, but Jesus gave us an assignment to do and a promise at the same time. Jesus commissioned us to make disciples of all nations and promised to be with us to the end of the age. Use any opportunity to represent Him.

In Matthew chapter ten, Jesus made an unfathomable statement.

Matthew 10:32-33

32 So everyone who acknowledges me before men, I also will acknowledge before my Father who is in heaven, 33 but whoever denies me before men, I also will deny before my Father who is in heaven.

Information leads to evaluation, evaluation leads to communication, and communication may lead to invitation. I will dig into this pattern in a later chapter.

Education

Education is more than just obtaining a degree. While degrees hold value, they do not inherently make a person truly 'good.' In a spiritual sense, education intertwines with discipleship and personal growth, teaching us the values of the faith that shape our essence and guide us to strive for goodness. This blend of learning nurtures our spiritual and moral development, which aligns with the principles of true 'goodness' in faith.

Jesus did not reward his disciples with a master's degree in teaching when training was done.

Jesus invested in the disciples to lead, teach, and preach. He didn't put up a sign inviting others to come to him; instead, he actively sought out people in need, such as orphans and the hungry. One of the most remarkable aspects of Jesus' teaching style was his personal interaction with his students, leading them by example. After preaching to large crowds, he would spend time with his disciples to discuss and reflect on the messages. Jesus was deeply involved in the lives of his disciples so they would, in turn, invest in others as well.

Just as Jesus taught and led, we, too, are called to teach and guide others in our community.

Philippians 2:3-8

"3 Do nothing from selfish ambition or conceit, but in humility count others more significant than yourselves. 4 Let each of you look not only to his own interests, but also to the interests of others. 5 Have this mind among yourselves, which is yours in Christ Jesus, six who, though he was in the form of God, did not count equality with God a thing to be grasped, seven but emptied himself, by taking the form of a servant, being born in the likeness of men. 8 And being found in human form, he humbled himself by becoming obedient to the point of death, even death on a cross."

To become like Christ is a lifelong development.

MEASURES

In a world saturated with false teachings intended to mislead and undermine the very foundations of God's truth, discernment has become essential. We are called to distinguish between what is good and what is evil, remaining steadfastly rooted in the Word of God. Every good and perfect gift, after all, comes down from the Father of the heavenly lights. Just as a compass provides direction and orientation in the wilderness, the Word of God serves as our ultimate guide, keeping us on the right path in both conduct and speech. Nearly three thousand years ago, a psalmist posed a question that remains as relevant today as it was in his time: **"How can a young man keep his way pure?"** The answer lies in the timeless wisdom of Psalm 119, which offers not only a guide for the young but for all believers, regardless of age. Its counsel provides the enduring foundation for a life of purity, faithfulness, and obedience to God.

Psalm 119:9-16.

⁹ How can a young man keep his way pure?

By guarding it according to your word. ¹⁰ With my whole heart I seek you; let me not wander from your commandments! ¹¹ I have stored up your word in my heart, that I might not sin against you. ¹² Blessed are you, O LORD; teach me your statutes! ¹³ With my lips I declare all the rules of your mouth. ¹⁴ In the way of your testimonies I delight as much as in all riches. ¹⁵ I will meditate on your precepts and fix my eyes on your ways. ¹⁶ I will delight in your statutes; I will not forget your word.

We are called to order our lives according to the Word of God, seeking Him continually, meditating upon and memorizing Scripture, offering Him sincere praise, and committing ourselves wholly to the Lord.

These are not casual suggestions but essential disciplines that must be embraced with earnest devotion and steadfast seriousness.

Let us pause and reflect on the methods we use and the implications that come with them.

Information is more than knowledge; it is an entry point into an intentional and Spirit-led conversation. A disciple of Jesus is not called to simply collect data, but to discern hearts. Information helps us meet people where they are, just as Christ meets us where we are.

As mentioned earlier, information leads to evaluation; evaluation opens the way to communication that acknowledges God, and communication can lead to invitation. That invitation draws us into education, not an education that seeks to impress, but one that transforms. True learning reshapes our hearts, teaching us to look beyond ourselves and to seek the good of others.

The journey of discipleship is a journey of surrender. We are called to empty ourselves so that Christ might fill us. Transformation into His likeness is not a momentary experience, but a continual becoming day by day, choice by choice, grace upon grace.

In the end, we must take faithful measures, practices that help us not only speak like Jesus, but live and walk as He did. For when our words and our ways align with His, the world begins to see the reflection of Christ through us.

On one of the mission trips to Albania, I had the assignment to coach youth soccer skills and create a tournament, in which all participants were supposed to put into practice the skills taught, in order to earn extra points.

Most of the students got carried away in the competition, neglecting the assignment given. In the end, some students from losing teams were rewarded, not because they lost, but because they fulfilled the assignment.

In life, we need to take measures that fulfill our goals. Obedience is a key measure in accomplishing the task given to us by Jesus.

Jesus had a goal and is still in the process. He wants us to continue what he has started. Make disciples of all nations.

The assignment for you and me is clear. I pray that we

"Explore the charts below for deeper insights and a clearer understanding."

INFORMATION
Entry point into intentional
and Spirit-led conversation

Helps us meet people
where they are, not
to collect data but
to discern hearts.

EVALUATION
Information leads to
reflection and discernment

Opens the way to
communication
that acknowledges
God

COMMUNICATION
Rooted in understanding
and compassion

Creates space for
invitation into deeper
relationship and faith

INVITATION
A call to education —
not to impress but to transfo

Encourages us to
look beyond ourselves
and seek the
good of othes

EDUCATION
True learning reshapes
the heart

A continual journey of
surrender and renewal

TRANSFORMATION
A continual journey of
surrender and renewal

Each step builds on the last, moving from gathering understanding to embodying Christ's character, forming a holistic cycle of Spirit-led discipleship.

Stage	Description	Spiritual Focus	Key Bible Verse(s)
Information	Entry point into Spirit-led conversation.	Awareness	"The fear of the Lord is the beginning of knowledge." Proverbs 1:7
Evaluation	Reflecting and discerning hearts	Discernment	"Test everything; hold fast what is good." 1Thessalonians 5:21
Communication	Speaking in ways that acknowledge God	Connection	"Let your conversation be always full of grace, seasoned with salt." Colossians 4:6
Invitation	Drawing others into relationship and growth	Openness	"Here I am! I stand at the door and knock." Revelation 3:20
Education	Transformative learning that reshapes hearts	Renewal	"Do not be conformed to this world but be transformed by the renewal of your mind." Romans 12:2
Transformation	Continual becoming, grace upon grace	Christlikeness	"And we all... are being transformed into his image with ever-increasing glory." 2 Corinthians 3:18
Faithful Measures	Living and walking as Jesus did	Witness	"Whoever claims to live in him must live as Jesus did." 1 John 2:6

APPLICATIONS:

Adding to Your Faith

After studying the *Main Objectives*, like identifying threats, Word of God Hasn't Changed, and disrupting false teaching, and after learning the *Methods*, like information, education, and faithful measures, it is time to apply what we've learned.

Applying God's Word confirms your identity in Christ. Faith is not complete until it is *lived*. The Apostle Peter calls us to grow in spiritual maturity, saying:

2 Peter 1:5–7 (ESV)

"For this very reason, make every effort to supplement your faith with virtue, and virtue with knowledge, and knowledge with self-control, and self-control with steadfastness, and steadfastness with godliness, and godliness with brotherly affection, and brotherly affection with love."

The ESV uses the word "**supplement**," while the KJV says "**add**." Both words mean *to supply abundantly, to build upon.* In contrast to the modern trend of *spiritual minimalism*, making faith comfortable or effortless, Peter challenges believers to *act intentionally and diligently.*

We have lowered our standards, withdrawn from our communities, and replaced relationships with advertisements and billboards. But Jesus *walked among people*. He *ate with sinners*. He *spoke truth in love*. He *engaged hearts face to face.*

Peter, once fearful, now restored, urges us to do the same: **"Make every effort."** Add to your faith. Let's look at what this means step by step:

1. **Add Virtue (Moral Excellence)**

    "For this very reason, make every effort..."

    Virtue is more than human morality; it is the *character of Christ*, faith, hope, and love lived out. True virtue reflects God's nature in our actions.

2. **Add Knowledge**

    Knowledge is *spiritual discernment*, wisdom that sees and assesses life through God's Word. Knowledge strengthens faith against opposition and helps us recognize truth from error.

3. **Add Self-Control**

    Self-control means governing thoughts, emotions, and behavior under the Spirit's authority.
    1 Corinthians 10:13 reminds us that "God is faithful... He will also provide the way of escape."
    Every temptation becomes an opportunity to exercise spiritual discipline.

4. **Add Steadfastness (Endurance)**

    Steadfastness is *active perseverance*. When trials arise, faith doesn't shrink; it grows stronger.

    Hebrews 10:36

"For you have need of endurance, so that when you have done the will of God.

You may receive what is promised."

5. Add Godliness

To be godly is to *be like God*. As Pastor Ken Adams of *Impact Disciples* teaches, a fully trained disciple reflects both the **character** and **conduct** of Christ. Godliness is not about perfection; it's about imitation of Christ in every area of life.

6. Add Brotherly Kindness

Brotherly kindness (Philadelphia) is family love—the affection believers share as members of one household in Christ.

1 Peter 1:22

"Having purified your souls by your obedience to the truth for a sincere brotherly love, love one another earnestly from a pure heart."

This love unites us beyond background, culture, or ethnicity.

7. Add Love (Agape)

Finally, the crown of all virtues—*love.*

If brotherly love reflects our bond, *agape love* reflects God's very essence. This love is sacrificial, deliberate, and unconditional.

1 John 3:18–19

"18 Little children, let us not love in word or talk but indeed and in truth. 19 By this we shall know that we are of the truth and reassure our hearts before him."

1 John 5:1

"Everyone who believes that Jesus is the Christ has been born of God, and everyone who loves the Father loves whoever has been born of him."

The Climb of Spiritual Growth

Steps	Add To...	Description	Key Verse
1	Faith → Virtue	Moral excellence; reflect Christ's character	2 Peter 1:5
2	Virtue → Knowledge	Spiritual understanding and discernment	Proverbs 2:6
3	Knowledge → Self-Control	Mastery of thoughts, emotions, and actions	1 Cor. 10:13
4	Self-Control → Steadfastness	Perseverance through trials	Hebrews 10:36
5	Steadfastness → Godliness	Living in reverence and imitation of Christ	1 Tim. 4:7–8
6	Godliness → Brotherly Kindness	Genuine affection toward believers	1 Peter 1:22
7	Brotherly Kindness → Love	Agape, sacrificial love, the essence of God	1 John 3:18–19

A Call to Alignment and Action

In this chapter, we searched deeply into our beliefs, examining whether our spiritual systems have become corrupted, and if they have, we are called to realign them with the teachings of Scripture.

We have learned that becoming like Christ is not a momentary achievement but a lifelong process. When our words and our ways reflect His truth, the world begins to see the image of Christ shining through us.

As citizens of His Kingdom, we are called to **talk like Him, walk like Him, and love like Him**

Yet, we recognize the growing gap between God and this world. Even within the church, compromise and apostasy have crept in. Christianity, in many places, seems to stand on the defensive, though here and there, small flames of revival still burn brightly.

Long ago, humanity turned away from God, but He did not abandon His people. Through the prophet Isaiah, God asked, *"Whom shall I send, and who will go for us?"* and Isaiah answered, *"Here am I; send me."*

Jesus reaffirmed that same divine mission in **Luke 19:10:**

"For the Son of Man came to seek and to save the lost."

That mission has not changed. The same question echoes through the ages today:

"Whom shall I send, and who will go for us?"

Will you be the one to answer, *"Here am I, Lord; send me"*?

27

Chapter Two
Who is to Go?

Unashamed: A Witness in Times of Freedom

A Personal Testimony

I grew up during the communist era in Romania, in the city of Beclean in Bistrița county, tucked within the mountains of Transylvania. Christianity did not come wrapped in comfort or convenience. It came with a cost.

As young believers, we organized visits to other churches across our region, traveling by bus, by train, or sometimes on foot. We brought our guitars, accordion, and our worn-out hymnbooks. We gathered for fellowship, to sing, to encourage one another, and to share the Word of God. And though persecution was harsh, our hearts were full. We lived for Jesus without thinking about the consequences, not because we were reckless, but because **Christ was worth everything**.

Every trip was a challenge. Our parents, from the little they had, paid for our food and transportation. We faced mockery from neighbors, insults from strangers, and threats from authorities. Many who cursed us came from an Orthodox background enforced by the state, where religion was cultural, not personal. Some even reported us to the police for disturbing public order simply because we were singing gospel songs.

But witnessing for Jesus wasn't a "program" we signed up for. It was **who we were**.

It was **who we represented**.

Faith wasn't private back then… it was visible, alive, and courageous.

From Persecution to Freedom

Now, decades later, freedom has come. The churches are open. The Bibles are printed legally. The fear has faded.

Yet something troubling has happened…

We have freedom.

But witnessing has become difficult.

We have comfort.

But the fire of evangelism flickers quietly.

We have open doors.

Yet many churches are closing theirs.

Is freedom no longer free?

Or have we simply forgotten what it cost?

We once risked everything to speak the name of Jesus.

Today, some are afraid to speak His name in public at all.

Where prisons once silenced believers, now indifference does.

Paul's Call Still Echoes

Paul writes:

⁷ For God gave us not a spirit of fearfulness, but of power and love and discipline. ⁸ Be not ashamed therefore of the testimony of our Lord, nor of me his prisoner: but suffer hardship with the gospel according to the power of God; ⁹ who saved us, and called us with a holy calling, not according to our works, but according to his own purpose and grace, which was given us in Christ Jesus before times eternal,

2 Timothy 1:7–9

If God has not given us a spirit of fear;

Why do so many believers live as if He has?

In a world where:

- hate speaks louder than love,
- marriage is no longer sacred,
- division replaces unity,
- and Christianity is treated as outdated.

There is an urgency to witness again.

Not out of guilt.

Not to check a box.

But because the world desperately needs the hope we have.

Today's Choice

I remember those days in communist Romania with gratitude. We were persecuted; yet we were bold. We had little, yet we shared everything. We were threatened; yet we rejoiced.

Perhaps…

Freedom did not weaken the Gospel,

But it has tested the courage of God's people.

The message I carry from my past into this moment is simple:

Do not be ashamed of testifying to what Jesus has done for the entire world.

Let us not trade bold faith for silent comfort.

Let us not let freedom become an excuse for fear.

Let us once again be witnesses;

not because we must…

But because Jesus is worthy.

Unashamed
A Witness in Times of Freedom

A FAITH THAT COST SOMETHING

During the communist era in Romania, Christianity was not a matter of convenience—it was a matter of conviction. As young believers, we trayeled from church to church throughout Transylvania to have fellowship, sing, encurage one another, and share the Word of God.

FROM PERSECUTION TO PERMISSION

Today, there is no secret police standing at the church door. No fear of being arrested for sharing Scripture, no restrictions on Bibles or open worship.

PAUL'S CHARGE STILL STANDS

Fear is not from God, Silence is not our ealling.

The Gospel is not a thing of the past.

A CALL FOR TODAY

We live in a time when what Jesus did for *emtire world*. Let us tise again with boldness. May freedom not silence us... but empower us.

For Christ is worthy of a courageous witness—now

A born-again Christian is called to be a witness. Before Jesus ascended to heaven, He made a powerful statement:

Acts 1:8

But you shall receive power when the Holy Spirit has come upon you; and you shall be witnesses to Me in Jerusalem, and in all Judea and Samaria, and to the end of the earth."

The phrase "shall receive" indicates a certainty and empowerment to witness.

Your testimony, expressing that you are saved, that you have repented, that you have received the Holy Spirit, and that you are obedient, makes you a witness.

As a follower of Christ, you should be prepared to share your faith, as stated in *1 Peter 3:15.*

But sanctify the Lord God in your hearts, and always be ready to give a defense to everyone who asks you a reason for the hope that is in you, with meekness and fear.

A follower of Christ may face challenges, including persecution. However, God has provided us with assurance and encouragement in *Matthew 10:19-20.*

19 But when they deliver you up, do not worry about how or what you should speak. For it will be given to you in that hour what you should speak;

20 for it is not you who speak, but the Spirit of your Father who speaks in you.

Sharing the Gospel is essential for making disciples of Jesus and fulfilling the Great Commission.

As a church, we embody the Bride of Christ. Therefore, we need to consider our priorities on a daily, weekly, monthly, and long-term basis. As a husband, father, and grandfather, I understand the importance of daily communication with my wife. If we see each other every day but only exchange words when I need something, our marriage will deteriorate quickly. Additionally, if I insist on seeing my grandchildren but neglect to connect with my children, the chances of maintaining a relationship with my grandchildren diminish significantly.

In a professional setting, one expects to receive payment in exchange for work performed. You cannot anticipate a salary without fulfilling your job requirements.

I believe we have a mandate that, for many years, has been neglected. When I served as a youth pastor, my focus was primarily on Bible study and worship. As a senior pastor, I concentrated on shepherding the congregation and preaching. As a pastor focused on missions, I prioritize equipping church members to share God's love with the world.

It's important to recognize that we cannot conduct church without worship, preaching, and fellowship within our home groups; however, we can easily overlook the most crucial mandate: witnessing to the lost.

According to **Mark 16:15**, Jesus is not presenting us with options but rather a clear mandate!

And He said to them, "Go into all the world and preach the gospel to every creature."

Who is to Go? Those who totally surrendered to Christ Jesus! Have you?

In many of my ministry years, I long to get closer to God and be a good servant. Most of these years, I was missing the importance and dedication to be and build Disciples. I trained leaders to serve our church communities, but something was missing. I started doing different Discipleship training programs, and they helped me in many ways, but one day, my good friend Mark Hobafcovich introduced me to Ken Adams, who is the founder of Impact Discipleship Ministries. A Godly man who not just walks the talk, but he's breeding discipleship. That was my **aha moment** when it comes to Discipleship.

When a lamp is plugged into a power source, it doesn't have to *try* to shine; it simply does, because it's connected to the source of electricity.

In the same way, when Jesus said, *"You shall receive power,"* He was promising that those who believe in Him will be connected to the source of spiritual power, the Holy Spirit.

That connection empowers believers not to struggle to witness but to *naturally shine* with the light of Christ through their testimony.

Who Is To Go?

This next chart summarizes the implications of accepting the call.

Receive Power:

- **Acts 1:8** "But you will receive power when the Holy Spirit comes on you; and you will be my witnesses in Jerusalem, and in all Judea and Samaria, and to the ends of the earth."

Be Witnesses:

- **1 Peter 3:15** "But in your hearts revere Christ as Lord. Always be prepared to give an answer to everyone who asks you to give the reason for the hope that you have. But do this with gentleness and respect,"

Face Challenges:

- **Matthew 10:19-20** "[19] But when they arrest you, do not worry about what to say or how to say it. At that time, you will be given what to say, [20] for it will not be you speaking, but the Spirit of your Father speaking through you."

Trust the Spirit:

- **Matthew 10:19-20**

Fulfill the Great Commission:

- **Mark 16:15 "He said to them,** 'Go into all the world and preach the gospel to all creation."

Your salvation, repentance, and obedience are like the lamp being plugged in and switched on. Once connected, you carry that light wherever you go, prepared to share your faith with others who are still in the dark.

Chapter Three
The Process

The process starts at the cross when Jesus died and paid in full for the sins of the world, and opened a door to all who believe, "The Door That Counts."

John 10:7-9.

7 So Jesus again said to them, "Truly, truly, I say to you, I am the door of the sheep. 8 All who came before me are thieves and robbers, but the sheep did not listen to them. 9 I am the door. If anyone enters by me, he will be saved and will go in and out and find pasture.

This conversation centers on Jesus preparing to return to His Father, emphasizing His unique role as the sole path to God. For anyone longing for eternal life with God, Jesus makes it clear there is only one way: through Him. He proclaims, "I am the door. If anyone enters by Me, that person will be saved and will go in and out and find pasture."

How do people find the way to God?

Jesus came to reconcile us with God, paid the price for all, and before ascending, gave His followers a strategy to continue His work. He affirmed His full authority, launched the Great Commission by outlining steps for sharing His message, and concluded with a great promise.

Every disciple's story begins somewhere. Imagine stepping into the shoes of a disciple, tracing their journey from the very first step.

The adventure does not start with a shout of "GO," but with a gentle "COME." "Come" is not a demand, but an open invitation. Before anyone can follow a command, they must first be shaped and prepared. To become a disciple of Jesus starts with a willing heart. Willingness means choosing a path and stepping through a doorway. That path and that door are found in Jesus.

Two foundational concepts should be considered before communicating the Christian doctrine of salvation to others.

1. Divine authority is absolute.

Matthew 28:18

And Jesus came and said to them, "All authority in heaven and on earth has been given to me."

Before His departure from the earth, Jesus made a powerful declaration that carries profound implications, not only for this world but also for the heavenly realms. He claimed full authority to rule over both heaven and earth. This divine authority calls for every person to willingly surrender to His lordship and to worship Him. As Scripture affirms:

Philippians 2:9–11

9 Therefore God has highly exalted him and bestowed on him the name that is above every name,

10 so that at the name of Jesus every knee should bow, in heaven and on earth and under the earth,

11 and every tongue confess that Jesus Christ is Lord, to the glory of God the Father.

Our Lord Jesus reminded His disciples of His supreme authority before ascending to heaven, where He now sits at the right hand of God. His declaration was not meant to intimidate them, but rather to assure them of His divine power and continuing sovereignty. It was a message of comfort, confidence, and reassurance that He reigns supreme, forever.

2. **The promise of continual divine presence is affirmed.**

Before Jesus told His disciples what to do, He first assured them of His sovereignty:

Matthew 28:20.

"And behold, I am with you always, to the end of the age."

Then, after giving them their mission, He offered them the greatest promise of all: **His continual presence.**

He did not say that He would be with them *only when needed* or *only in times of trouble.* Instead, He declared, **"I am with you always."**

What an assurance! What a promise! Jesus Christ is with every believer permanently, guiding, strengthening, and comforting us through every season of life.

The same process Jesus did with his disciples has to be done to every believer.

Building upon these principles, Jesus provided his followers with a systematic approach to perpetuate his ministry. Entering into the Christian faith typically follows a sequence: Come first, which leads to acceptance, which then leads to surrender.

COME – ACCEPTANCE – SURRENDER

Our adventure began with a simple call: Come and see!

Assessment: Where do you find yourself along your path?

Where are you on this journey?

Steps	Notes on your journey progress
Come and See	
Come and Follow	

Come and Remain	
Come and Go Out	

Jesus did not conclude the process of spiritual development after the initial step, 'Come and see,' nor after the subsequent steps, 'Come and follow,' and 'Come and Remain.' The process reached completion when the Holy Spirit filled the disciples. Possessing knowledge alone is insufficient. Understanding the 'how' is important; discerning the 'way' is essential. The Holy Spirit provides guidance regarding the 'where,' 'when,' and 'how.'

Curiosity may prompt acceptance of the invitation to 'Come and See,' and companionship may encourage following. However, only genuine commitment enables one to 'Come and Remain.' Experiencing life with Christ empowers individuals to accept the call to 'Go.'

How is your experience walking with Christ? Are you listening to his call?

Remember, the One who has all power and authority is with you and the center of all you do.

The Great Commission authority belongs to Jesus, and he promised to be with us.

The Journey of a Disciple: From "Come" to "Go" ⟶

Stage	Invitation / Command	Description
1.Come and See	*John 1:39* "Come, and you will see."	The initial invitation sparked by curiosity and openness to Jesus.
2.Come and Follow	*Matthew 4:19* "Follow Me, and I will make you fishers of men."	A call to commitment, leaving old ways behind to walk with Jesus.
3. Come and Remain (Abide)	*John 15:4* "Abide in Me, and I in you."	Deepening relationship through continual communion and dependence on Christ.
4. Be Filled with the Holy Spirit	*Acts 1:8* "You will receive power when the Holy Spirit has come upon you."	Empowerment through the Spirit to live and serve as Christ did.
5. Go and Make Disciples	*Matthew 28:19–20* "Go therefore and make disciples of all nations."	The outflow of discipleship, participating in Christ's mission.

Spiritual Focus	Key Scripture	Mark of Maturity
Awareness – Encountering Christ personally.	John 1:35–46	Curiosity becomes faith.
Obedience – Learning from His example and teaching.	Matthew 4:18–22	Daily choice to follow Jesus' lead.
Intimacy – Being transformed by abiding in His presence.	John 15:1–11	Spiritual stability and fruitfulness.
Empowerment – Walking in spiritual authority and discernment.	Acts 2:1–4	Spirit-led life and discernment.
Mission – Sharing Christ's life and message with others.	Matthew 28:16–20	Multiplying disciples through love and witness.

Chapter Four
The Message

When I was young, one of my dreams was to have a guitar and to learn how to play.

That was not my only dream. As a young boy growing up, I loved the University of Craiova Soccer club, and I envisioned playing for that club one day. Unfortunately, as part of an evangelical family, the system was not friendly to us. Becoming a soccer player was a push to think too far. For my sixteenth birthday, I had the biggest surprise when my brother, Nicu, and my father, Simion, handed me a guitar. There was an obstacle with that as well. I had no one to teach me until one day a sister of a family friend came to town, and she was a great musician. She wrote the schematics and how-to on five pages, and that did it for me.

Learning guitar was central to my life. Playing and singing Godly songs that I learned from my mom led me to accept Christ as my savior. This story may not mean a lot to you, but it means everything to me. God appointed the right person at the right time. I started this chapter with my story for a good reason. Have you heard the expression "Meeting them where they're at"

My story is a good example of someone who found me where I was. Someone was listening and willing to help out. It heartened me when she tuned the guitar at the point of taking it from her hands. She could have just said, That's it. She did not judge me for my actions but rather took time to explain how it works. When my twelve-string guitar was tuned, and she started playing it, I was like, "I want to be as good."

When engaging in a first-time conversation with someone, paying close attention to details can make a significant difference in how the interaction unfolds. Witnessing to others is not just about sharing words; it is about connecting with the heart, understanding their journey, and creating a safe space for dialogue. Here are some key principles that can guide this process:

- **Practice active listening**: Truly listening goes beyond hearing words; it means observing body language, tone, and emotional cues. Ask thoughtful questions, reflect back what you hear, and ensure the person feels understood. This shows that you care about their experience, not just delivering a message.

- **Avoid judgment and criticism**: Every person comes from a unique background, with their own struggles and perspectives. Responding with judgment or criticism can close off communication and foster defensiveness. Instead, focus on empathy and compassion, recognizing the person as a child of God.

- **Demonstrate sincere understanding**: When people feel genuinely understood, they are more likely to open up about their fears, doubts, and questions. Vulnerability is often the first step toward spiritual growth, and your patient, non-condemning presence can create that opportunity.

- **Build a foundation of respect**: Respect is essential in any meaningful relationship. Respecting someone's journey, their pace, and their choices helps create trust and invites them into a dialogue rather than a lecture. This foundation can become the starting point for a potential spiritual journey together.

Meeting someone where they are requires a Christ-like character. It involves humility, patience, and intentional effort to connect on a deeper level. The goal is not to force change but to reflect Christ's love through your words, actions, and attitude. By embodying these principles, you can foster genuine relationships that may eventually lead to spiritual transformation.

You'll find a Christ-like character in *Galatians 5:22-23.*

22 But the fruit of the Spirit is love, joy, peace, longsuffering, kindness, goodness, faithfulness, 23 gentleness, self-control. Against such, there is no law.

Every individual comes with a distinctive background, a unique educational journey, and a variety of environments that influence their life experiences.

Assessing the "What is about to happen" is extremely important. If it is a coworker, classmate, or neighbor, someone you know a little about, prepare yourself before sharing your testimony. Write down a short version of your testimony so you can deliver the message efficiently.

I will present a series of approaches and guidelines for effectively navigating these diverse settings. Let's explore the importance of customizing people's professional paths and daily lives to meet them where they are at.

There are so many ways to approach unreached people with the Gospel, yet so many Christians are not comfortable doing it. Where or how do we start a conversation?

Below are a few conversation breakthrough templates, based on people's professions or whereabouts.

Templet # 1

Sharing God's Word with a Pharmacist's Approach + The Door That Counts

1. **Begin with Prayer**

   Before approaching anyone, pray that God will **soften their heart** and make them open to the Gospel.

2. **Start the Conversation Naturally**

   You: Hello John/Joy, if I'm not mistaken, you're a pharmacist.
   Them: I sure am.

   You: I've always believed that it is a great profession; congratulations!

   (Pause to listen to their response.)

3. Make a Connection Between Their Work and God's Work

You: What I appreciate about your profession is that you have a similar approach to people as God does.

Them: How so?

You: Just as you assess individual symptoms to create a tailored regimen for healing, God looks at each person's life and offers a path for spiritual healing. In Matthew 9:35, it says:

"Jesus went through all the towns and villages, teaching in their synagogues, proclaiming the good news of the kingdom and healing every disease and sickness."

You: Just like you tailor medicine to someone's needs, Jesus tailors His care and guidance to each person's heart and life.

4. Introduce the Gospel Clearly

You: That's why I created a simple way to share the Gospel called **"The Door That Counts."** It's a quick, visual explanation that helps people understand salvation.

- **Why we need God:** Humanity's fall brought judgment on all of us.
- **God's solution:** Jesus Christ, the Son of God, paid the penalty for all who believe in Him.
- **Personal testimony:** I've experienced His love and transformation in my life, and that's why I follow Him.

You: Just like you wouldn't give the same medicine to everyone, God has a personal plan for each person. And He invites us to experience His healing personally, spiritually, and eternally.

5. Leave the Door Open

If they're not immediately open:

- Be **friendly and patient.**
- Keep in touch and build **real friendships** because many come to Christ through relationships.
- Avoid pressure, **clarity, kindness, and your personal testimony** often open doors more than arguments.

You: I'd love to keep this conversation going sometime, maybe over coffee, if you're interested. No pressure: just sharing what has changed my life.

This approach combines:

- A **personal connection** (Pharmacist analogy)
- **Scripture reference** for credibility
- **Clear Gospel explanation** (Door That Counts)
- **Gentle, relational follow-up**

The next two pages display the "Door That Counts" example card. The front shows an image, while the back explains its meaning with descriptive text.

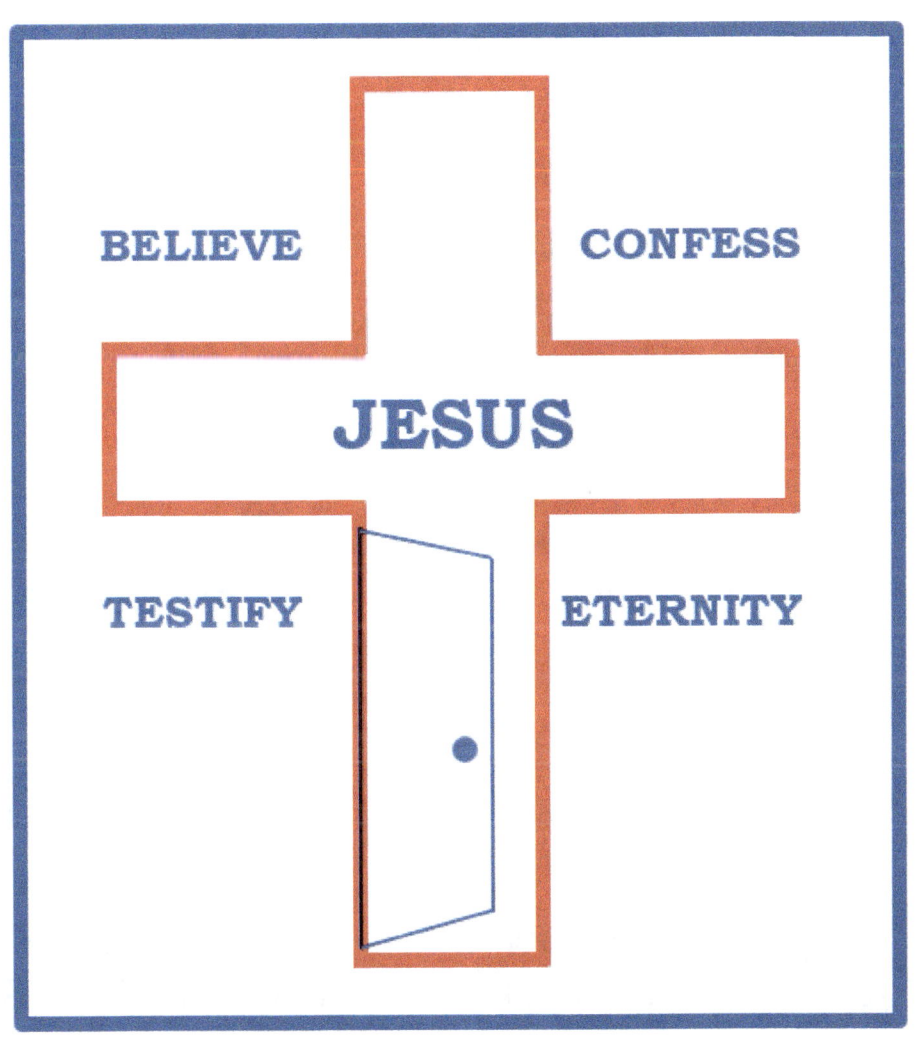

"The Door That Counts"

God was in great harmony with the man He created, but something happened along the way.

Wickedness results in separation from God.

Romans 6:23. For the wages of sin are death, but the free gift of God is eternal life in Christ Jesus our Lord.

Jesus restored our relationship with God, but: You must:

1. **Believe.** *John 5:24.* Truly, truly, I say to you, whoever hears my word and believes him who sent me has eternal life. He does not come into judgment but has passed from death to life.
2. **Confess.** *1John 1:9.* If we confess our sins, he is faithful and just to forgive us our sins and to cleanse us from all unrighteousness.
3. **Testify.** *Romans 10:9.* Because, if you confess with your mouth that Jesus is Lord and believe in your heart that God raised him from the dead, you will be saved.
4. **Eternity.** *John 3:36.* Whoever believes in the Son has eternal life; whoever does not obey the Son shall not see life, but the wrath of God remains on him.

Dear God, I am a sinner, but today I believe that Your Son Jesus Christ died on the cross for my sins and He rose again. Please come into my heart and help me live for you.

Amen

I'm adding a few more templates, with the Idea of meeting people where they're at.

Template # 2

Quick Construction Approach Script

1. **Friendly opener:**

   You: Hi John/Joy! I hear you're in the construction business, right?
   John/Joy: Yes.

   You: That's awesome! It's a job that takes real skill and wisdom. I really respect that.

   (Pause, listen, build rapport.)

2. **Bridge to spiritual insight:**

   You: You know, what I admire is that your work is a lot like how Jesus talks about life.

   John/Joy: How do you mean?

   You: Just like you start a building on a strong foundation, Jesus said a wise person builds their life on Him, so when storms come, everything stands firm.

3. **Scripture connection:**

   You: In **Matthew 7:24-27,** Jesus talks about a wise man who built his house on the rock. The storms came, but the house didn't fall.

Those who ignore His words are like someone building on sand; the house falls when storms hit.

You: Basically, a strong foundation matters in construction and in life.

4. **Invitation / Application:**

You: God wants us to have a solid foundation, too. If we build our lives on Him, we can stay strong through anything. Would you like me to show you a simple way to start building that foundation today?

(This is where you can lead into the "The Door That Counts" Gospel presentation method.)

This version keeps it **friendly, relatable, and short enough for casual conversations** without losing the core message.

Matthew 7:24-27.

Everyone therefore that heareth these words of mine, and doeth them, shall be likened unto a wise man, who built his house upon the rock: 25 and the rain descended, and the floods came, and the winds blew, and beat upon that house; and it fell not: for it was founded upon the rock. 26 And everyone that heareth these words of mine, and doeth them not, shall be likened unto a foolish man, who built his house upon the sand: 27 and the rain descended, and the floods came, and the winds blew, and smote upon that house; and it fell: and great was the fall thereof.

Follow-up Steps (as recommended after Template #1):

- Offer to pray with them.
- Give them a small card or scripture reference they can keep.
- Encourage ongoing conversation and friendship.
- Be patient and respectful if they're not ready to respond immediately.

Template # 3

Sharing God's Word with a Teaching Background Approach

You: Hello, John/Joy, if I'm not mistaken, you are a professor.

John/Joy: I sure am.

You: I've always believed that teaching is one of the most influential and important professions. Congratulations on your work!

(Pause to listen to their response, acknowledge it, and engage naturally.)

You: One thing I really appreciate about your profession is that you have a similar approach as Jesus did—very direct, yet effective in guiding others.

John/Joy: How so?

You: Jesus was profound, yet He taught in a way that everyone could understand. Just as you correct and guide your students, Jesus corrected and guided those around Him. He was known as a teacher from God. We see this story in the book of John:

John 3:2 (KJV)

"The same came unto him by night, and said to him, Rabbi, we know that thou art a teacher come from God; for no one can do these signs that thou doest, except God be with him."

Transition:

After this, you can gently steer the conversation toward God's message using the same steps you follow in Template #1:

1. **Listen actively** – Ask about their teaching journey or philosophy.
2. **Share a personal connection** – Relate a moment in your life where God's guidance helped you understand or grow.
3. **Invite reflection** – Ask if they have ever seen spiritual parallels in their own teaching.
4. **Offer a next step** – Suggest reading a short passage, attending a Bible discussion, or simply praying together.

The key principle here is **tailoring your approach**: you respect their profession, relate their experience to Jesus' methods, and naturally guide them toward the spiritual lesson.

Template # 4

Medical/Healthcare Professional Approach

You: Hello John/Joy, if I'm not mistaken, you are a doctor/nurse/healthcare professional.

John/Joy: I am.

You: That is such a noble and life-changing profession. You literally help people in their most vulnerable moments.

(Pause and listen.)

You: What I really admire is that your work reminds me of how Jesus healed and cared for people, not only physically but also emotionally and spiritually. Just like you diagnose and treat illnesses, Jesus healed hearts and souls. He was known as a compassionate healer and teacher.

Luke 4:40 (KJV)

"Now when the sun was setting, all they that had any sick with divers diseases brought them unto him; and he laid his hands on every one of them, and healed them."

Transition:

You can then ask how they see the connection between physical and spiritual healing and share how God's Word brings wholeness to both body and soul.

Template # 5

Business/Entrepreneur Approach

You: Hello John/Joy, if I'm not mistaken, you run a business or manage an enterprise.

John/Joy: Yes, that's right.

You: I've always believed business is one of the most influential ways to impact lives—through leadership, vision, and stewardship.

You: What I find inspiring is that your work reflects principles Jesus used in leadership and stewardship. He taught about managing resources wisely, leading people with integrity, and building for the long term.

Matthew 25:14-16 (Parable of the Talents, KJV)

"For the kingdom of heaven is as a man travelling into a far country, who called his own servants, and delivered unto them his goods..."

Transition:

You can ask if they ever consider spiritual values in leadership decisions and gently introduce how God's Word offers wisdom in guiding people and resources.

Template # 6

Artist/Musician/Creative Approach

You: Hello John/Joy, if I'm not mistaken, you are an artist/musician/creative professional.

John/Joy: Yes, I am.

You: That is such a beautiful and influential profession. You have the gift of inspiring people and expressing what words sometimes cannot.

You: I see a parallel between your work and Jesus' teaching. He communicated profound truths in ways that everyone could understand and connect with, much like an artist conveys emotions and truths through their creations.

John 1:3-4 (KJV)

"All things were made by him; and without him was not any thing made that was made. In him was life; and the life was the light of men."

Transition:

You can explore how creativity reflects God's own creativity and how the beauty in their work points to deeper truths in life and spirituality.

Template # 7

Construction/Engineering Approach

You: Hello, John/Joy. If I'm not mistaken, you are in construction/engineering.

John/Joy: I am.

You: That's a remarkable profession! You literally build the foundation for others' lives, quite like architects of the future.

You: I find it fascinating that your work is similar to how Jesus builds spiritual foundations. He teaches people to build their lives on solid truth and wisdom, just like you ensure structures are solid and safe.

Matthew 7:24-25 (KJV)

"Therefore whosoever heareth these sayings of mine, and doeth them, I will liken him unto a wise man, which built his house upon a rock..."

Transition:

You can then discuss how life's foundation can be tested, just like buildings, and share the importance of a spiritual foundation in Christ.

Reflections

Chapter One: Counterintelligence

- **Main Objectives:** As we reflect on these objectives, I urge you to live like Jesus, love like Jesus, and walk like Jesus.
- **Methods:** Obedience is a key measure in accomplishing the task gave it to us by Jesus.
- **Applications:** When our words and our ways reflect His truth, the world begins to see the image of Christ shining through us.

Chapter Two: Who is to Go - That connection empowers believers not to struggle to witness, but to *naturally shine* with the light of Christ through their testimony.

Chapter three: The Process - Remember, the One who has all power and authority is with you and the center of all you do.

Chapter four: The Message - For the wages of sin are death, but the free gift of God is eternal life in Christ Jesus our Lord.

Recommended Resources

impactdisciples.com

The curriculum of Impact is a walk in Jesus' daily life, in who He was and what He did. Here are a few resources from Impact Disciple Ministries:

- Disciple Making Church, seminar
- Disciple Making Pastor, seminar

Curriculum for Impact Groups:

- Disciple Making Essentials
- Character of Christ
- Conduct of Christ
- The making of 315 Leaders

Works Cited

"Penn Jillette." AZQuotes.com. Wind and Fly LTD, 2025. 22 November 2025. https://www.azquotes.com/quote/627845

What makes this book different is its emphasis on meeting people where they are. John shows us how to share faith with compassion and authenticity, just as Jesus walked among people and spoke truth in love. Every point is grounded in Scripture, and he writes with pastoral warmth and honesty, sharing what he's learned through decades of ministry.

Mark Hobafcovich

www.ingramcontent.com/pod-product-compliance
Lightning Source LLC
Chambersburg PA
CBHW071200130626

46555CB00004B/1526

* 9 7 9 8 9 0 2 2 4 0 3 0 3 *